Best Advice

40 leadership tips from 40 leaders

compiled by

John D. H. Greenway & Nicole Linger

Published in 2014 by Mercuri Urval

Mercuri Urval Limited
Third Floor South
35 Portman Square
London
W1H 6LR

T +44 (0)20 7467 3730

Best Advice

40 leadership tips from 40 leaders

Forewords

40 Leadership Tips

Best Advice

40 leadership tips from 40 leaders

Happy Birthday

1974!

It was the year that ... ABBA won the Eurovision Song Contest with "Waterloo" ... Bjorn Borg, at just 18, won the French Open, the first of his 11 Grand Slam single titles ... Volvo brought out the 240 and 260 Series ... Mercuri Urval was established in the UK. All were great Swedish exports.

This book celebrates the 40 years since Mercuri Urval set up business in the UK market. When I was asked how we should celebrate the occasion, this book was the second thing that came to my mind after ... "Let's have a party!"

This is a book with 40 authors - we have simply compiled it. We posed a simple question to 40 leaders from different organisations across diverse sectors: "What has been the best leadership advice you have received?" Each of these leaders has had some association with Mercuri Urval.

We all need advice at times. The "best advice" helps us to make sense of the situation and enables us to make the best informed decisions. What is more, it also helps us to become better decision makers as it provides us with insight and not just information. This approach is right at the very heart of the Mercuri Urval business concept.

I want to thank all 40 contributors for their participation in this project. All proceeds from the book will be given to City Gateway, an outstanding charity dedicated to improving employment opportunities for young people in Hackney, one of the poorest Boroughs of London.

The following 40 capsules of best advice could be analysed, categorised or critiqued but each has been a relevant, memorable and practical gem to the writer. As you read and reflect, I hope that you find the 40 best advice tips stimulating and insightful. May you be better prepared for the next time somebody asks for your advice!

John D.H. Greenway

john.greenway@mercuriurval.com

So, **what's with the oranges?**

When Mercuri Urval was established over 40 years ago what we did was new, different and even misunderstood. To help explain what we did we told a story about oranges.

The story simply described how an orange picker looked at a basket of oranges but he found that although they all looked the same on the outside, they could be very different on the inside. Furthermore, it was not enough just to know which oranges were sweet and which were sour or dry. The orange picker could only pick the right orange for his customer if he really knew what the customer planned to do with it.

The same principles can be applied to understanding people and organisations. They also reflect the beliefs on which Mercuri Urval was founded and which have guided us for over 40 years. How can organisations make sure that they have the right people to deliver the right results?

In that time we have had the privilege of working with some incredibly dynamic and forward thinking people; clients, colleagues and candidates. We would like to take this opportunity to thank them all for their collaboration and support.

We have been lucky enough to work with some world-class projects and clients, ranging from the long held dream of creating tunnel access between Great Britain and France, to enabling Olympic events deliver an exceptional performance. Additionally, we have helped many entrepreneurs accelerate the international expansion of their businesses.

Whilst our tools, methods and skills have developed and been adapted to the changing needs of clients, the fundamental belief behind all that we do and the starting point for all our work and advice remains same. If you match the *right* people, to the *right* job at the *right* time then results are so much easier to achieve. If it was only so easy when picking oranges!

Stephen Finley

Managing Director, Mercuri Urval UK

A **Bedouin** dictum

There is an old Arab saying from the times when they roamed the harsh desert lands of Arabia in the fifth century.

The sentence is a kind of palindrome and was intended as a pun to teach a point. It states: "The Lord of a people is their servant." It can also be read as: "The servant of a people is their Lord."

To me, this Bedouin dictum encapsulates the essence of leadership. Leadership is about serving all the stakeholders in a company: serving the owners by pursuing a strategy that delivers sustainable profitability; serving the employees by empowering them to achieve the best they can by trusting their ability and allowing them to make decisions and serving the clients by giving them an exemplary product.

Saker Nusseibeh

Chief Executive, Hermes Fund Management Limited

30
years
old

I was 30 years old and recently appointed to the board of Ronson plc. The Chairman was a very experienced City professional called James Roe.

I was discussing a particular issue with James and told him that there was some action I was about to take that I feared would make me unpopular.

In reassuring me that I was taking the right course, James simply said: "Christine, never forget the most popular person in an organisation is often the biggest fool!"

I have never forgotten this and I find myself frequently quoting James' advice.

In any leadership role, we are all faced with some difficult decisions which will never please everybody. Focus on the facts and give clear direction, rather than worrying unduly about whether everyone will be happy with the decision...they rarely will.

Christine Hodgson

President, Capgemini UK

Flip it

My undergraduate degree was a combined major in music composition and stage directing. My directing professor was a deeply insightful man. Although I worked harder and harder, my first three plays stunk, each getting progressively worse. After the third disaster, my professor asked me how I felt. I told him I was sizing up different bridges.

"How much time do you spend studying the script?" he asked.

"Hundreds of hours," I answered.

"How much time do you spend casting?"

"A day."

"Flip it."

My next play was entirely different. Because I only had one day to study the script, I had to rely on the actors' interpretations. I had to focus on them: their motivations, their ideas, and the dynamics between them.

The result?

They delivered an inspiring performance. As for me, I learned the essence of leadership.

Matt Wenger

CEO, Think Tank

Every morning and **every** evening

Sir Brian Smith, then Chairman of Metal Box, was one of my early business mentors. Leaders are, amongst many other things, responsible for the prudent growth of their companies. When I was concerned, as an adviser to Metal Box, that they might be paying a full price for what turned out to be a quality company, Brian said to me: "James [he probably actually said "James, lad"], it is better to pay slightly too much for a high quality business than it is to pay a lot too little for a poor quality one."

And when I sought his counsel the day in February 1995, after the bankruptcy of Barings: "Talk to your staff, every morning and every evening. They all have mortgages and families to worry about and you must give them something positive to take home at the end of the day."

We did that during the ten days before we were rescued by ING and in the following 18 months, we lost one member of staff out of 150 across Europe and were the No.1 UK M&A adviser in 1995, the year of our bankruptcy.

James Lupton
Chairman, Greenhill Europe

1960s

The best advice I received was from the first consultancy company I met. They were appointed to review the police vehicle workshops in the late 1960s.

In answer to a question the lead consultant said, "If you think we are here to solve your problems you are wrong. We are here to help you understand what they are and offer advice on how best to resolve them."

Keith Hellawell

Chairman, Sports Direct
and a former Chief Constable

Seeing is
believing

The best advice I have received has always been in the form of observed action not words - closely observing the really effective leaders I've worked with over the years - the ones I've most admired, working out what it is they do and how they do it and then putting it into practice.

I'm still learning in this way. In fact I'd say I've learned and absorbed more as I've become a more experienced and practiced leader myself. At some point in my career, this learning moved from an unconscious to a conscious activity and I only wish that transition had been earlier as it amplified and accelerated the learning process.

Stephen Beynon

Managing Director, British Gas Business

Embedding
a **new value**

I gained a great deal of inspiration in 2007 when I met Al Gore, former Vice President of the United States, at a conference in Europe. His opening address built upon the excellent documentary 'An Inconvenient Truth'. It helped me understand that to embed a new value within a company requires bold leadership – to never be satisfied.

By being resolute at Skanska, we have carved out a reputation as one of the UK's leading green companies. We have differentiated our offering, discovered a real business opportunity and attracted exceptionally talented people. Perhaps best of all, we continue to make a positive contribution to society – that makes me feel good.

Mike Putnam

President, Skanska UK

The **mirror** effect

I was given simple, but transformational advice by my teacher, Patrick Russell, whilst I was a postgraduate, studying conducting at London's Royal Academy of Music.

The advice was this:

Consider the effect of your leadership as if you were looking into a mirror, whether conducting a choir or directing a business. The characteristics that you display will be reflected in those you are leading.

And indeed, I have found that when I am tense or feeling underprepared or frustrated, this is also evident in my choir's performance.

Conversely, when I strive for high standards and am joyful and confident, I see this mirrored in their performance, producing the passion, boldness and commitment that I am looking for.

Rachel Staunton

Founder and Director of the London Youth Choir

Negotiation lesson

"L'important n'est pas d'avoir raison, mais d'avoir satisfaction."

"Don't try to be right, but focus on satisfaction."

I was posted in Eastern Europe in the early nineties, in a development role for a large utility. I was negotiating the terms for a large acquisition and not making progress for days. With these few words, my boss, a former political advisor to the French President, set me back on track. Re-assessing what was in it for each party involved, terms could then be agreed rapidly.

This is all about the balance between the task, the team and the individuals. Basically, it is more important that the whole team gets to the set destination, rather than forcing each individual in the team to set his/her feet in exactly the same tracks.

Laurent Bermejo

Deputy Chief for Europe, Bureau Veritas

Words
we often
forget

It's a difficult question to answer as there has been so much advice along the way. I guess I'd go back to my days at Boots the Chemists when I first joined the senior management team. I suddenly found myself with a group of peers who had previously been nothing short of heroes, really talented people for whom I had the utmost respect. Inevitably my confidence in this stellar group was low and I struggled to really hit the ground running.

Until one of them, someone I knew less well, took me to one side and gave me a piece of advice I still hold today:

"Remember Ted – you are no greater than any man... nor any less."

It is the last three words that we often forget.

Ted Smith

Chairman, Embrace Group

A **powerful** question

Over a decade ago in a leadership training session the professor asked me a powerful question in front of my whole management team: "What is the most important thing a leader should do?"

I answered: "Show direction and motivate with a clear mission, vision and strategy." Feeling very confident with my answer, the professor came to me and said: "No. It is asking questions."

Since then I have always remembered to ask questions, listen and seek to understand the answers. When you have a business challenge or if there is a problem somewhere in the organisation, just go to the responsible people one by one and start asking open questions. After a while they have all told you what the problem is, how to solve it and what they are going to do to solve it. Thus they are then highly motivated to solve the problem, because they themselves identified the problem, told the boss about it and in addition, came up with the solution.

Hans Sohlström

President and CEO, Rettig Group

Listen to my instincts

I keep coming back to something my father told me at the age of 18.

"Don't be too cerebral about it" he said.

At the time I was selecting which University to apply for. His point was that I had done all the research and had the facts I needed to make the decision. I had logically thought through each option, but it was time to step away from the detail and listen to my instincts.

I have spent most of my career in Engineering and Technical companies where decisions are supported by data and logic. As I have moved into more senior roles I have reminded myself when it is time to stop looking for the data to provide the answers. It is then that I remember my father's words and I allow my judgement to play a part too.

Vicki Potter

Group HR Development Director
Oxford Instruments

The **secret** blend

Creating a top performing team is not simply an amalgam of a number of bright, enthusiastic and creative people. The secret is in selecting the right blend of different but supportive individuals who not only understand the strengths each of them bring, but are also open about their own deficiencies and proactively seek, as well as give, support and mentorship within the team.

When such openness, trust and collaboration have been created, its collective skill set can be harnessed powerfully and successfully in pursuit of the shared goal.

Dave Wickham

CEO, Vtesse

Few
of
us

Few of us ever come to work to do a poor job for our employers.

When we do something badly we feel the pain without being told and yet some managers simply focus on the individual's failings and rarely either compliment them or acknowledge the many times that the person has done the job consistently well.

A focus on just the poor side of a performance leaves an employee feeling deflated, unappreciated and lacking in confidence even though 90% of their work may be of a high standard.

Regular, well meaning words of praise for the good work of an employee often results in them wanting to constantly aspire to do better and better for their manager and the team. It also boosts their confidence and that, in turn, results in a higher level of performance.

It helps to produce proactive, highly motivated teams and much improved results for all.

Gerard Hay
Managing Director, Abena UK

Brink of complacency

The best advice I have received was the need for a leader to have constant "restless dissatisfaction."

At the time I was running a service business with strong growth and profitability, with a 47% market share. My team and I thought we were doing a great job but we were, in truth, probably on the brink of complacency. I took the advice as a challenge. I set about looking at the business from a more detached point of view and followed the maxim that managers work "in" the business and leaders work "on" the business. Over the next two years, we increased our market share by 70% which reflected the true potential of an already successful business.

Of course, you can't always project "restless dissatisfaction" to your staff. You can, however, build their capability to achieve stretch targets, inspire and align their efforts and reward achievement of milestones along the path.

Keith Bushnell

CEO, HCML

Don't be the first

Do the right thing. Set the colour, look and shape of what you want. Stand back, give both power and permission. Get people on the bus. Manage poor performance. Be brave, be yourself, be a spectator and at the same time be a player too. Concentrate on your super strengths and employ for your weaknesses. Control your diary, not vice versa. Be human: believe in people and not process and get things done through people and not process. Be prepared to cut deeper and quicker when you have to. Be concerned to control only what you can control. Most of all don't be who you are not. Don't be the first to speak in a meeting - everybody knows you are the boss; there is no need to show it. Don't be concerned if you don't have all the answers, enjoy watching your team come up with them.

Paul Thandi

CEO, NEC Group

They will **surprise** you

Take Risks - If someone is 75 percent right for a role, stretch them, give them a chance and they will surprise you!

Stay Connected - Strive to be uber-networked and immersed in your market. Double up on context with all stakeholders; it's easier for everyone to get aligned.

Empower - Identify the 20 percent of tasks that consume 80 percent of your time. Empower your team to take responsibility for the remaining 80 percent.

Balance your life - Take an hour of a sport every day; it will help you rejuvenate. And don't forget your family – it's easier to find a good job than a good husband!

Julie Woods-Moss

SVP for Marketing & Global Accounts,
Tata Communications

Deep into your soul

It is easy to be a leader: but it is hard to be a great leader.

To do so involves digging deep into your soul and giving those for whom you are responsible the depths of your being. So many leaders are tinny and insubstantial: they smile, stand and talk well, but there is nothing inside. If there is nothing inside, there is nothing to give.

To truly transform others and the institutions we lead, leaders themselves have to be transformed. They have to lead out of the depths of who they are.

Anthony Seldon

Political Historian and Master at Wellington College

Friends and enemies

My father advised, "If you treat a perceived enemy like an enemy they will definitely become an enemy. Treat someone as a friend and they will probably become a friend."

Concentrate on the things that make a real difference to the company, the rest will normally sort itself out.

Fix what you must fix to succeed not just what you can fix.

Average people working well together is far better than excellent people not working together.

To progress in business make yourself redundant by recruiting great people.

If the people at the top do not know where the company is going and do not work together, the whole company will go nowhere and not work together.

John Mould
Chief Operating Officer, HMFL

The push factor

The art of leadership is knowing when to push hard to accelerate change or progress and when to step back and allow change and progress to emerge at a natural pace from within the team. You cannot push all the time as the rate of change would be unsustainable BUT you do need to determine when to push to ensure the team reaches its potential.

Chris Halbard

EVP & President, International,
Synchross Technologies

My Grandfather

The best advice I ever received came from my Grandfather, who had a 50 year career in the construction business. On the day I started my first role leading a large number of people, he told me to always imagine myself sitting on 'the other side of the desk' whenever I was about to act or take a decision.

He felt that this helped you to understand how you would feel in the other person's shoes and how you would react and to use that insight to determine whether what you are proposing is reasonable, fair and right.

His advice has always stood me in good stead.

Peter Gowers
CEO, Travelodge

The
Knowledge

When you are working in B2B you must build up long relationships with your employees and customers; you always must keep your promises and always know what you are talking about which means knowledge. It is always better to say "I don't know, but I will find out and come back to you tomorrow"... and do that. Knowledge does not come to you; only you can create it!

Erik Frisell
CEO, Audicom Pendax

Opening minds

Mahatma Gandhi said: "Be the change you want to see in the world."

Leadership is about constant anticipation of and preparation for the future. Today is the past tomorrow – leadership is opening minds for people so they understand what is expected from them in pursuit of future goals. In that change process, leadership is also being brave enough to say goodbye to those who cannot make it and contribute to the future state. At the same time onboarding, retaining and developing the right talent so they can always embrace new challenges and step up both as individuals and in teams.

Kenneth Molgaard-Pedersen
Global Head of Executive Search & Talent Management, People & Culture, Vestas

Scottish pithy advice

The best pithy advice I have received to date:

"Keep the heid while others are losing theirs" (That means "keep calm" in Scots!)

"It's all about the people"

"Make the relationships work and the rest will follow"

Barbara Anderson

Non-Executive Director at
Hydrogen Group PLC, Monodraught Ltd and
London Waste and Recycling Board

Never forgotten it

"Spend your time doing what you do best. Understand your weaknesses but don't waste time trying to improve them. Play to your strengths. Delegate your areas of weakness to others."

This was advice given to me by Mike Welton, later CEO of Balfour Beatty, around 1986 in my annual appraisal. I have never forgotten it and passed it on to many as I think leaders waste a huge amount of time and effort trying to improve their weaknesses when they could be making a real difference by deploying the skills that they are strong in.

David Fison

CEO, Osborne

Radiators and Drains

You can teach most people most things except enthusiasm. So I always look for enthusiastic people, first knowing that any gaps in their skills can be quickly remedied. Enthusiastic people are by their nature positive and full of ideas. But that can't be learnt so you need to seek these people out. There is a great phrase, "You are either a radiator or a drain" and drains tend to suck the life out of an organisation.

John Pike

Founder and Managing Director,
The Forty Percent Symposium

From Max's head to Max's desk

In 2005 I was CEO of a Welsh-based holding company who held some great global patents in the electrical products and distribution sector.

I was a frequent monthly visitor to our Turkish JV partners. On one such visit, I sat with Max, the Managing Director, debating how we could add a "top control box" to a new electrical cabinet design destined for future use in naval and shipbuilding markets.

Max took a pencil from his top pocket and sketched what the top box would look like. After 15 minutes we came up with something that would fit the bill. I turned to Max and said, "Great, could we have a prototype made for our meeting next month?" Max looked at me and said – "Next month?"

He called his engineering design manager to his office and they huddled around this sketch.

40 minutes later the engineering manager returned to Max's office, and to my complete astonishment placed the prototype on Max's desk. He had CAD/CAMed the design, broke into the manufacturing MRP system and produced the prototype in 40 minutes flat.

From Max's head to Max's desk in 40 minutes.

On the flight back to the UK (complete with the prototype) I thought how fast-to-market innovation is a way of life for Max.

Mark Coia

Managing Director, Mabey Bridge,
Renewables, Energy & Marine Division

Everybody
is a genius

At the beginning of my first ever Headship, somebody quoted Albert Einstein to me:

"Everybody is a genius.

But, if you judge a fish by its ability to climb a tree,

It'll spend its whole life believing that it is stupid."

I was leading a team of staff in a small school in a very socially deprived area of London. I wanted staff to have high expectations of our children and ensure that the children are at the centre of every decision we make.

We have been on an incredible journey. Our aim is to make sure there are no invisible children in our school and, in fact, that all children fly, whatever their particular strengths may be.

Jenny Parris

Headteacher, Mary Magdelene School

Initial
mentor

One piece of advice that I took from my initial mentor, Richard Shord many years ago...

"Your number one job as a leader isn't to motivate people but rather to avoid de-motivating them." I think about this often when I'm aiming to give candid, helpful feedback.

Like all good advice I don't always heed it....

Martin Holt

Chief Executive, Bellrock

Without hesitation

I am not sure I can say, at least not definitively, what the best leadership advice I have received is. Advice is, and has always been, welcome. What I can say though, without hesitation, is that I have valued other people's example more than anything else; my father's in particular. His leadership is relational, humble, vulnerable, transparent, honest and faithful. I don't just want to follow my father, I want to be like him.

My father also helped me to think about who I wanted to be and how I wanted to live. He taught me most, if not all, of the leadership advice I needed to know before I needed to know it; through our relationship, through conversation, through questioning, but most of all, through his example.

David Plummer

CEO, Freetricity

The
elephant

"Don't try and swallow the elephant in one go...split large challenges into bite-sized chunks and delegate where possible!"

Earlier in my career I was given an opportunity to start and lead a new business for a large multinational technology company. Having made an excellent start generating over 400% of the annual revenue target in just 9 months and recruiting team members to deliver the programme, as a junior leader I felt I was expected to try to do everything myself and keep issues and service delivery within the team. In a 1:1 my boss at the time who ran the UK & Ireland business, quickly identified my challenge as I underestimated the magnitude of the service delivery challenge that lay ahead. His advice was "Don't try and swallow the elephant in one go" and instead to split out the delivery elements into smaller workflows and then delegate to the wider business team ......otherwise I would sink!

Martin Hook

Managing Director, Alma Consulting Group UK

Potential to be **bigger**

My most enlightening moment was when I was advised by my HR Director, in a large financial organisation, to seek out the most diverse range of talent in order to attract and develop the highest performing team; to look for people who had potential to be bigger than me and always find ways to include people rather than reasons to exclude them.

Later, my CEO told me to look for people with passion, energy, edge and execution and I have, over the years, become very good at spotting talented people who I have developed.

My network still includes these stars who I have had the pleasure to see grow, work with and watched securing successful high profile roles in leading organisations. I am really proud of them and I know that my success has been down to my high performing teams.

Denise Keating

Chief Executive,
Employers Network for Equality & Inclusion

Brain and heart

When you speak to your people as their manager, talk to their brain.
When you speak to them as their leader, talk to their heart.

Albert Nußbaum

Chairman, Mercuri Urval Central Europe

Easy to get lost

When you work for an organisation the size of BT, it's easy to get lost in a multi-billion dollar, global business. Over the years I've unearthed valuable insights that have helped me to become a better leader, peer and friend to the hundreds of colleagues I work with daily.

At BT we not only value diversity but we actively seek to integrate different cultures into our organisation to enrich each individual, team and the company as a whole. Career progression is based on meritocracy; and empowerment is the norm. We remind every BT employee, no matter what their role that our success is dependent on the capabilities of an individual as well as on each person's ability to contribute his life's skills and experience to the success of the group.

Kevin Taylor

President,
BT Asia, Middle East and Africa and Global
Logistics

It's **got** to be **emotional**

Often individuals in leadership positions fail to recognise the difference between management and leadership. They default to managing their teams in the misguided belief they are leading.

Management is comprised of the necessary processes and systems to run an efficient team and is born of pragmatism and necessity. Leadership is about building strong relationships, motivating, inspiring and releasing the discretionary performance in individuals. It is an art, not a science and is born of emotion and belief.

Leadership has got to be emotional and if you don't feel emotion when you lead, then you are probably managing.

John Steele

CEO, Youth Sport Trust and Chairman, English Institute of Sport

Expecting too much?

As a Junior Manager I was once bemoaning the performance of my sales team to my Director and said, "Perhaps I am expecting too much."

His reply was, "Never lower your expectations; as a leader strive for perfection and if you come up a little short then you won't have done too bad."

It was a great piece of advice and something I have always carried with me. Maintaining high standards can be difficult, but if you are clear and consistent with your expectations, then your team will always know where they stand and will generally follow.

Steve Playford

Global Director, Financial Times

Complex and confounding

There have been many learning experiences in my 35 years in business – some great, some painful. The consistent theme has always been people; those you work with, those you work for and your customers. Interventions that have been most impactful have come from leaders who took the time to understand me as an individual, help me see my strengths, understand my impact on others, appreciate the need for confidence balanced with humility and a relentless focus on execution.

So what did all of that teach me? Well, however complex and confounding the business environment is that you operate in, it is crucial for success to focus on three core elements:

- Establish a clear, relevant business process; a vision and associated goals that are ambitious and understood by the people in your business. They must be able to relate to them, be motivated, rewarded, and measured against the attainment of them; meeting commitments is central to success.

- Employ the best people you can; no matter how good a leader you think you are, it is the abilities and qualities of those you lead who will determine the success of your business; understand them, provide them with the support they need and reward them well.

- Communicate – be clear, consistent and honest with your customers, stakeholders, staff and especially your board.

Above all, always be yourself...

Peter Ellingworth

CEO, ABHI

Whenever **troubles** come **our way**

A key part of the leadership journey is being able to lead with the knowledge that you are going to face difficult challenges and situations along the way and not allowing these difficulties to wear you down or defeat you, but instead to shape you into a better leader.

Developing a positive mind-set about the fact that hardships will always come and actively using them to improve who you are and how you lead, enables you to lead better and with greater humility, whatever the circumstances.

In the Bible, the book of James explains that whenever troubles come our way, we should let them be an opportunity for joy, because when we are tested our endurance has a chance to develop and grow.

If we are able to achieve this then we can become stronger, greater and crucially, more humble leaders.

Eddie Stride
CEO, City Gateway

Soldiers I have travelled with

When I was at University I was an Army Officer. The best leadership advice I received was from the soldiers I travelled with in the lorries on the way to exercises. They were not looking for an Officer to be a friend, to be popular or to be funny. The best leaders, they said, were fair and consistent. A leader should have no favourites, should set out their values and principles and then should abide by them and be completely fair in overseeing them with the team. It is not about being popular, it is about being fair.

Will Carling

*Owner, WCM and
former England Rugby Captain*

Throughout history

A number of years ago, I was given some advice on the importance of being a courageous leader.

Throughout history, almost every instance of leadership that has delivered progress – whether in business, politics, military, or sport – has involved having the courage needed to overcome obstacles that appear along the way. Leaders need courage to step outside of their comfort zones; to make tough decisions; to drive through change; to place their trust in those they manage and then to hold them to account effectively. It is courage that takes you from knowing what is needed, to taking action... even when you know it will be uncomfortable or unpopular. This is what fosters trust and sets the right example for others to follow.

I have often reflected on this, and it has encouraged me as I've faced my own obstacles.

John Pettigrew

Executive Director, National Grid

A
Scandinavian
Retrospective

As Mercuri Urval first started in Sweden in 1967, it is my privilege to write some concluding comments to this short book.

More than 45 years ago, Mercuri Urval was created to help to answer a simple but important question: How can organisations make sure that they have the right people in place to deliver the best possible results? By answering this question over the years we have built strong partnerships with our clients and together we have learned the importance of having the right leadership capabilities in place.

Mercuri Urval were amongst the pioneers stating that leadership matters and that leadership is defined by results. It is about envisioning, engaging and executing the purpose and direction of an organisation - and it all happens in a relational environment. This means that true leadership requires followers and emphasises that leadership is a behaviour and not a formal role. As a consequence leadership is a function of a person's capabilities – some inherited (emerging over time) and others are learned through experience - and some Best Advice.

I want to give my thanks to all the contributors for providing such a diverse and fascinating range of "Best Advice" for developing true leadership.

Finally, I send my congratulations to all my UK colleagues on the 40th birthday of Mercuri Urval UK!

Hanne Pihl

Managing Director, Mercuri Urval Sweden

Made in the USA
Charleston, SC
02 September 2014